Rookie
Read-About® Science

Liftoff!

By Carmen Bredeson

Consultants

Minna Gretchen Palaquibay
Rose Center for Earth and Space
American Museum of Natural History
New York, New York

Nanci Vargus, Ed.D.
Primary Multiage Teacher
Decatur Township Schools
Indianapolis, Indiana

Katy Kane
Educational Consultant

SCHOLASTIC INC.
New York Toronto London Auckland Sydney
Mexico City New Delhi Hong Kong Buenos Aires

Designer: Herman Adler Design
Photo Researcher: Caroline Anderson
The photo on the cover shows the launching of the Space Shuttle *Endeavour*
at Johnson Space Center, Houston, Texas.

ISBN 0-516-24490-6

12 11 10 9 8 7 6 5 4   4 5 6 7 8 9/0

Printed in the U.S.A.   61

First Scholastic paperback printing, June 2004

Launch day is almost here for the space shuttle. When the space shuttle launches, it will be sent into space.

The shuttle is pulled into a huge building.

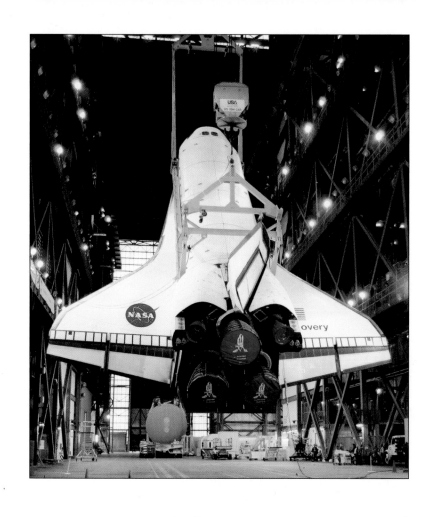

Cranes lift it up so it
is pointed to the sky.

A fuel (FYOO-uhl) tank is attached to the shuttle. The fuel will give the shuttle power.

On either side are two rocket boosters. The rocket boosters give the shuttle extra power.

fuel tank   rocket boosters

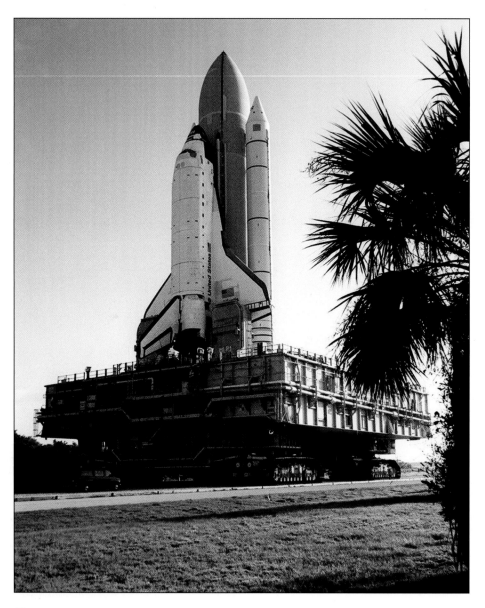

It is time to go to the launch pad. The shuttle is carried on a big, flat truck. The name of the truck is crawler.

Crawler moves like a tank. It moves on big belts with cleats. The cleats grip the ground and help move the heavy load.

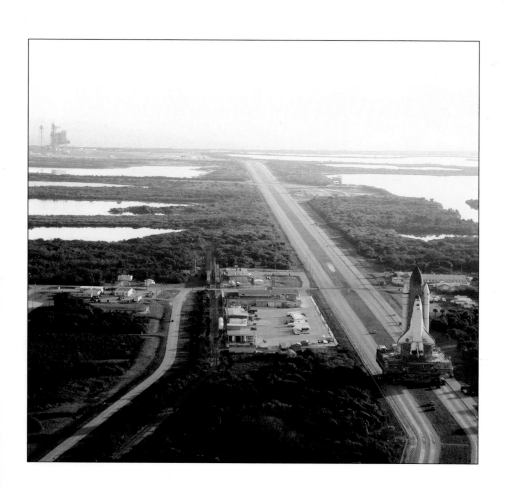

Crawler goes about one mile an hour. It takes the shuttle almost five hours to get to the launch pad.

The astronauts (AS-truh-nawts) are also getting ready for liftoff. They put on their orange launch suits. A van is waiting to drive them to the shuttle.

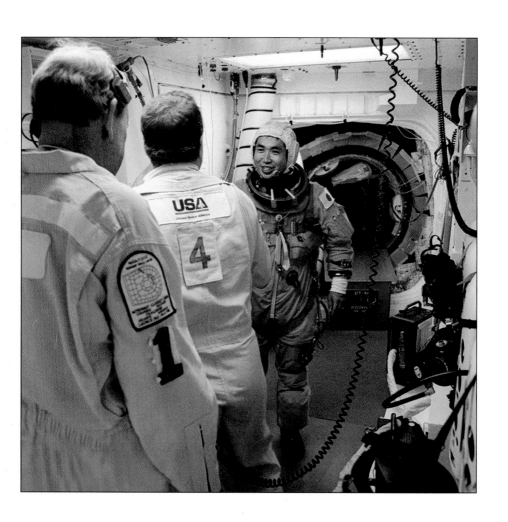

The crew gets in an elevator (EL-uh-vay-tur) at the launch pad. They ride up to the shuttle door.

The astronauts crawl through the door. Helpers strap them into their seats. Then, the helpers leave the shuttle and close the door.

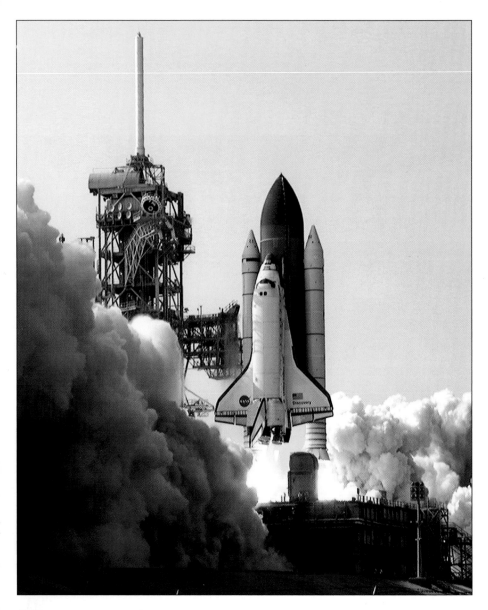

Everyone is ready. The main engines start six seconds before liftoff. The noise from the engines gets louder and louder.

Five, Four, Three, Two, One, Liftoff!

The shuttle begins to shake. Flames shoot from the bottom.

The astronauts are pushed back in their seats. Up they go, faster and faster. For eight and a half minutes they take a wild ride.

Suddenly, it is calm and quiet again. The engines have shut down.

The shuttle is going around Earth.

The astronauts unbuckle their belts. They float out of their seats. They are all grinning from ear to ear.

Words You Know

astronaut

fuel tank

launch pad

launch suit

rocket booster

space shuttle

Index

About the Author

Carmen Bredeson has written dozens of nonfiction books for children. She lives in Texas and enjoys traveling and doing research for her books.

Photo Credits